AF228348

COUNTRIES
ON THE
WORLD STAGE

SPOTLIGHT ON

Russia

Tracy Sue Walker

Lerner Publications ◆ Minneapolis

For Mom and Dad

Read by an expert reader.

Copyright © 2024 by Lerner Publishing Group, Inc.

All rights reserved. International copyright secured. No part of this book may be reproduced, stored in a retrieval system, or transmitted in any form or by any means— electronic, mechanical, photocopying, recording, or otherwise—without the prior written permission of Lerner Publishing Group, Inc., except for the inclusion of brief quotations in an acknowledged review.

Lerner Publications Company
An imprint of Lerner Publishing Group, Inc.
241 First Avenue North
Minneapolis, MN 55401 USA

For reading levels and more information, look up this title at www.lernerbooks.com.

Main body text set in Aptifer Sans LT Pro Semibold.
Typeface provided by Linotype AG.

Illustration on page 11 by Laura K. Westlund.

Designer: Athena Currier
Lerner team: Sue Marquis

Library of Congress Cataloging-in-Publication Data

Names: Walker, Tracy Sue, author.
Title: Spotlight on Russia / Tracy Sue Walker.
Description: Minneapolis : Lerner Publications , [2023] | Series: Countries on the world
     stage | Includes bibliographical references and index. | Audience: Ages 8–12 | Audience:
     Grades 4–6 | Summary: "Stretching from eastern Europe to northern Asia, Russia is the
     world's largest country. Discover Russia's landscape, economy, and people. Then learn
     about its history and look to the country's future"— Provided by publisher.
Identifiers: LCCN 2022046215 (print) | LCCN 2022046216 (ebook) | ISBN 9781728492025
     (library binding) | ISBN 9798765602584 (paperback) | ISBN 9781728496702 (ebook)
Subjects: LCSH: Russia (Federation) —Juvenile literature.
Classification: LCC DK510.23 .W35 2023 (print) | LCC DK510.23 (ebook) | DDC 947—dc23/
     eng/20220923

LC record available at https://lccn.loc.gov/2022046215
LC ebook record available at https://lccn.loc.gov/2022046216

Manufactured in the United States of America
1-53141-51151-2/8/2023

TABLE OF CONTENTS

INTRODUCTION

A New Nation

ON DECEMBER 25, 1991, THE RED FLAG OF THE UNION OF SOVIET SOCIALIST REPUBLICS (USSR) CAME DOWN FOR THE LAST TIME. The flag's gold hammer and sickle had been a symbol for communism. But when the nation broke up into fifteen separate countries, the old flag of Russia was restored. The flag with stripes of white, blue, and red rose, signaling the start of a new nation, the Russian Federation (Russia). Russia would be a republic in which people would have more freedoms than they did in the USSR. It was a change for the nation and the world.

The Russian flag flies again on December 25, 1991.

CHAPTER 1

The Russian Empire

For two hundred years, the Mongols invaded and ruled the land now known as Russia. The Mongols were a nomadic and tribal group from central Asia. It wasn't until 1480 CE when Ivan III, the grand prince of Moscow, freed Russia from Mongol rule that the country united.

In 1547 Ivan IV became Russia's czar. A czar rules a country and is similar to an emperor or empress. Ivan IV forcefully formed the Russian state.

Ivan IV ruled as Russia's czar from 1547 to 1584.

He is often called Ivan the Terrible because of the violence he caused. After his death, there were years of fighting within Russia.

The fighting stopped when Mikhail Romanov was elected czar by other nobles in 1613. Mikhail started the Romanov dynasty, which ruled Russia for over three hundred years. Peter the Great came to power in 1682. He reorganized the government. He gave local governments more power. A central government was created to handle foreign and domestic business. When Peter's armies defeated Turkey and Sweden, the Russian Empire became a world power.

Russia gained more control over their southern border. Under Catherine the Great, Russia also became known for its arts and education.

Mikhail Romanov started the Romanov dynasty, which ruled Russia for over three hundred years.

After Catherine's reign, French emperor Napoleon Bonaparte invaded Russia and war began in France. In 1914 Russia was again involved in a European war called World War I (1914–1918). Russia's ally, Serbia, was attacked. Russia, Serbia, France, Britain, Italy, and the United States fought against Germany, Austria-Hungary, Bulgaria, and the Ottoman Empire. But Russia's military had many losses. The Romanov dynasty ended in the revolution of 1917, which led to Vladimir Lenin and the Communist Party taking power. The war ended in 1918, and Russia gave up land to Germany and Poland. After a difficult civil war, the USSR was organized in 1922.

Explore Russia's Landscape

Covering about 6.6 million square miles (17.1 million sq. km), Russia is the largest country in the world. It spans two continents, Europe and Asia. Russia makes up one-tenth of all land on Earth.

Russia has different types of landscapes. The southern portion of Russia has rolling plains called steppes. The most northern parts are in the cold tundra. Siberia covers 75 percent of Russia. This area is covered by pine forests called taigas.

ATLANTIC OCEAN
GREENLAND
CANADA
Alaska (US)
This map does not reflect the true size of all countries
NORTH POLE
ARCTIC OCEAN
Bering Sea
NORWAY
FINLAND
ESTONIA
LATVIA
Moscow
BELARUS
UKRAINE
Black Sea
GEORGIA
Caspian Sea
RUSSIA
ARCTIC CIRCLE
Sea of Okhotsk
AZERBAIJAN
KAZAKHSTAN
CHINA
Sea of Japan
CHINA
MONGOLIA
NORTH KOREA
PACIFIC OCEAN
ARCTIC OCEAN
NORTH AMERICA
EUROPE
RUSSIA
ASIA
ATLANTIC OCEAN
AFRICA
PACIFIC OCEAN
PACIFIC OCEAN
SOUTH AMERICA
INDIAN OCEAN
AUSTRALIA
SOUTHERN OCEAN
Country capital
International border
Mountains

THE TRANS-SIBERIAN RAILWAY

The Trans-Siberian Railway is almost 6,000 miles (9,656 km) long. It is the longest railroad on the planet and connects Russia. Czar Alexander III came up with the idea for the railroad. Construction of the railway started in 1891. Almost ninety thousand people helped build the railway, which was completed in 1916. In modern times, the Trans-Siberian Railway helps people travel and move goods across Russia.

From the western city of Moscow to the southeast city of Vladivostok, the Trans-Siberian Railway connects Russia.

Over 145 million people live in Russia. There are about 120 ethnic groups and over one hundred languages spoken in Russia. Many Russians trace their ancestry to the Slavs who settled the area over fifteen hundred years ago.

CHAPTER 3

A Changing Economy

As part of the USSR, Russia had a centralized Communist economy. The government decided how much things cost and how much people were paid. It also owned all the businesses. From 1928 to 1940, USSR dictator Joseph Stalin took small farms from the people who owned them to make them into large state-run farms. He thought this would help farms grow more crops. Instead, fewer crops were produced, and many people died because there wasn't enough food.

In 1939 the USSR entered World War II (1939–1945). Stalin and the country allied with Germany. Germany didn't have much money after World War I. Dictator Adolf Hitler and the Nazi Party used people's anger over the economy to spread hate about people who were different from them. They targeted groups such as Jewish people, and about six million Jewish people were killed during the war. In 1941 Germany attacked the USSR. The USSR, Britain, the United States, and other countries fought against Germany and its allies. The USSR and its allies defeated Germany in 1945.

As part of the Cold War (1947–1991), the USSR and the US competed to see who had better spaceflight. The USSR launched the satellite Sputnik in 1957. It was the first Earth-orbiting satellite.

After the war, the USSR and the US began arguing. The US was angry that the USSR was spreading communism. The USSR worried that the US had atomic weapons and that it opposed communism. The US and the USSR each wanted to have more power to defend themselves. This led to the Cold War. The Cold War wasn't an actual war between the USSR and the US, but it was a time of very high tension between the two countries, and it did lead to smaller wars and conflicts.

In 1985 Mikhail Gorbachev became the leader of the USSR. Gorbachev began summit talks with US president Ronald Reagan. These talks brought the Cold War to an end. It also helped change the USSR's economy. Before, the government owned all the country's resources, set prices for products, and decided when and how many products would be made. After the Cold War, businesses were given more control, and the prices and number of products made depended on how many people were buying or selling them.

Gorbachev received the Nobel Peace Prize in 1990.

People walk outside a mall in Moscow.

In 1991 Boris Yeltsin won Russia's first presidential election. He supported democracy. Finally, on December 25, 1991, the Communist state was dissolved and the USSR became the Russian Federation. The nation was made up of small republics that are similar to states. Businesses in Russia gained some freedom from the government. Russia began trading more easily with other countries.

OIL AND NATURAL GAS INDUSTRIES

Russia's economy relies on fossil fuels. Russia is the world's third-largest oil producer and the second-largest producer of natural gas. Russia sends its oil to China and countries in Europe, especially Germany, the Netherlands, and Poland, through pipelines.

In 2021 Russia produced about eleven million barrels of oil per day.

Forestry is an important industry in Russia. Russia is one of the world's leading log and lumber producers and exporters. Because of the country's enormous size, nearly 20 percent of the world's forestry resource is found in Russia.

Even though much of Russia's land does not produce crops, agriculture is still an important part of its economy. Wheat is the country's most important crop, and Russia is the world's largest exporter of wheat. Other important agricultural products are sugar beet, milk, barley, sunflower seeds, and maize.

A forest in Pashiya, Russia

CHAPTER 4

The Federation and Politics

When the USSR dissolved in 1991, Russia became one of fifteen former Soviet republics to become independent. Russia went through the difficult transition from a Communist dictatorship to a capitalist democracy.

Russia has three branches of government that are supposed to act independently of one another: executive, legislative, and judicial. The executive branch is headed by the president. The president appoints the prime minister,

who then appoints the cabinet members. Members of the cabinet oversee government ministries such as the Ministry of Foreign Affairs and the Ministry of Defence.

The legislative branch is made up of the Federal Assembly, which has two houses. The lower house is the State Duma, and the upper house is the Federation Council. The State Duma has 450 members who are elected and serve five-year terms. The Federation Council has about 170 members from Russia's various states. The judicial branch is made up of the courts. The highest courts in Russia are the Constitutional Court and the Supreme Court. The president proposes judges for these courts, and they are then appointed by the Federation Council.

PRESIDENT OF THE RUSSIAN FEDERATION

The president is the most powerful person in the Russian government. Presidents are the Supreme Commander-in-Chief of the Armed Forces. The president is supposed to make sure that the constitution of the Russian Federation is followed. The constitution contains the principles and laws by which Russia is governed. The president also decides the country's policies. Citizens elect the president for a six-year term by secret ballot. But some experts think that the elections are not honest and that outcomes are controlled by those in power. The president lives in the Grand Kremlin Palace in Moscow.

In 2004 Vladimir Putin was elected to his second presidential term. After that term, he had to leave office due to term limits. But then Putin won presidential terms again in 2012 and 2018. Many of Putin's actions have led people to believe he is a dictator rather than a president. Early on, Putin was able to stabilize Russia's failing economy and gain popular support. This allowed him to make changes to the government that gave him more power. The Russian election and political process is tightly controlled. There is almost no room under the new dictatorship for opposing political parties.

Alexei Navalny is a lawyer and activist. He led the Russia of the Future party, an opposition party that challenged Vladimir Putin's United Russia party. Navalny wrote about Russia's corruption on his blog. In August 2020, Navalny became very ill from poisoning. Experts appointed by the United Nations Human Rights Council said the Russian government was responsible for the act. Navalny kept speaking out. In March 2022 Navalny was sentenced to nine years in prison. Many believe that Navalny is being punished for speaking out about the government.

Alexei Navalny (*front center*) marches with supporters in 2017.

Current Events

IN 2022 RUSSIA ATTACKED A NEIGHBORING NATION, UKRAINE. Ukraine was part of the USSR, and Russia wanted it to be part of Russia. The Russian government said it was only attacking military areas, but the country then also attacked public areas such as schools and museums. People in Russia who protested the war were arrested. Later that year, Russia drafted men to fight in the war. Tens of thousands of men left the country so that they would not have to fight.

Russia's population has been decreasing over the years. The population fell by 430,000 people during the first five months of 2022. That was before thousands of men fled the draft. The Russian government has been forcing some people from Ukraine into Russia. People are worried that Russia is trying to erase Ukraine's culture.

Vast numbers of migrants have also left Russia in recent years. Allowing and encouraging greater immigration could increase Russia's population. However, the country's fear and treatment of immigrants has led to many immigrants living in poor conditions or being forced into detention camps.

Russian men enter neighboring Kazakhstan after leaving Russia in 2022.

People work on a pipeline that Russia uses to export its gas.

Russia depends greatly on its gas and oil exports to European nations, but more nations are turning to green energy in the face of climate change. After its invasion of Ukraine in February 2022, other countries placed sanctions on Russia. These sanctions have negatively impacted Russia's economy. In the years to come, Russia must figure out ways to strengthen its already declining economy and population. Many are watching and waiting to see how recent events such as Russia's war in Ukraine will affect Russia's standing on the world stage.

879	Kievan Rus, the first major East Slavic state, is founded.
1237–1240	Mongols invade Kievan Rus.
1547–1584	Ivan IV, or Ivan the Terrible, rules as the czar of Russia.
1613	Mikhail Romanov becomes czar, and the Romanov dynasty rules for three centuries.
1682-1725	Peter the Great rules as czar of Russia.
1762-1796	Catherine the Great serves as empress of Russia.
1914	Russia enters World War I.
1917–1918	The Russian Revolution takes place, and Lenin's Communist Party comes to power.
1927	Joseph Stalin becomes a dictator, and Russia becomes a military power.
1939	Russia enters World War II.
1991	After a vote, the Soviet Union is dissolved.
2022	Russia invades Ukraine.

RUSSIA FAST FACTS

Official name: Russian Federation (Russia)

Population: 146,078,887

Land area: 6,592,850 square miles (17,075,400 sq. km)

Largest city: Moscow

Capital city: Moscow

Form of government: federation and semi-presidential republic

Official language: Russian

Flag:

GLOSSARY

agriculture: the growing and harvesting of crops and the raising of livestock

culture: the beliefs, social practices, and characteristics of a certain society, group, or place

economy: the process or system by which goods and services are made, sold, and bought in a country

election: the act or process of choosing someone for public office by voting

export: something that is sent to another country to be sold

fossil fuel: a fuel that is formed in Earth's crust from dead plants or animals. Coal, oil, and natural gas are fossil fuels.

pipeline: a line of connected pipe that is used for carrying liquids, such as oil, over a long distance

sanction: an action taken to force a country to obey international laws by limiting or stopping trade

tundra: a large area of flat land in the northern parts of the world where there are no trees and the ground is always frozen

LEARN MORE

Britannica Kids: Russia
https://kids.britannica.com/kids/article/Russia/345773

Cool Kid Facts: Russia Facts
https://www.coolkidfacts.com/russia-facts/

Doeden, Matt. *A Look at Ukraine*. Minneapolis: Lerner Publications, 2024.

Gottschall, Meghan. *Zdravstvujtye, Russia*. Ann Arbor, MI: Cherry Lake, 2021.

Kiddle: Russia Facts for Kids
https://kids.kiddle.co/Russia

Layton, Christine. *Travel to Russia*. Minneapolis: Lerner Publications, 2022.

National Geographic Kids: Russia
https://kids.nationalgeographic.com/geography/countries/article/russia

Sabelko, Rebecca. *Russia*. Minneapolis: Bellwether Media, 2023.

INDEX

PHOTO ACKNOWLEDGMENTS

Image credits: The Asahi Shimbun/Getty Images, p. 5; Fine Art Images/ Heritage Images/Getty Images, p. 7; Universal History Archive/Universal Images Group/Getty Images, p. 8; Wikimedia Commons PD, p. 9; Artem Svetlov/ Wikimedia Commons (CC BY 2.0), p. 12; Universal History Archive/Getty Images, p. 14; Aleks49/Shutterstock, p. 15; Peter Turnley/Corbis/VCG/Getty Images, p. 16; Massimo Borchi/Atlantide Phototravel/Getty Images, p. 17; NATALIA KOLESNIKOVA/Getty Images, p. 18; Alexander Chazov/EyeEm/Getty Images, p. 19; council.gov.ru/Wikimedia Commons (CC BY 4.0), p. 21; Askin Kiyagan/Anadolu Agency/Getty Images, p. 23; Evgeny Feldman/Wikimedia Commons (CC BY-SA 4.0), p. 24; AP Photo, p. 26; Bair175/Wikimedia Commons (CC BY-SA 3.0), p. 27; Nataliya Borysenko/Shutterstock, p. 29.

Cover: Makar Surkov/Getty Images.